HANDLING THE PRESSURE

ISBN 978-0-9891591-2-8

All scripture referenced from NKJV.

P.O. Box 30250, Anaheim, CA 92809-0208
888-644-8811
ktt.org

LIFE IS FULL OF PRESSURE. We all struggle with handling pressure. Maybe you can relate to the man who had enough of being an adult as he felt the pressures of life piling up:

> *"I am hereby officially tendering my resignation as an adult. I have decided I'd like to accept the responsibilities of a six-year-old again. I want to go to McDonald's and think that it's a four-star restaurant. I want to see who can blow the biggest bubble. I want to think that M&M's are better than money because you can eat them. I want to drink Kool-Aid and eat Lemonheads with my friends. I don't want to change my clothes because they got a little dirty.*
>
> *I want to enjoy every day like it's a summer vacation. I want to return to a time when life was*

simple. All you knew was to be happy because you were unaware of all the things that should make you worried or upset. I want to be excited about little things again, like my new Hot Wheel or jump rope. I want to live simply again. I don't want my day to consist of computer crashes, paperwork, cleaning, children, chores, depressing news, illness, and loss. I want to be in the roller derby and believe that The Three Stooges are real.

So, here's my checkbook, my car keys, my credit card bills, my 401(k) statements, my cell phone. Okay, I'll keep that. And not least of all, my mortgage book! I'm officially resigning from adulthood. And if you want to discuss this further, you'll have to catch me first. Tag, you're it. See you later, alligator."[1]

We can all identify with that, can't we? On a given day, many of us would happily accept the responsibilities of a six-year-old because life can become so burdensome, draining, and busy that we no longer feel alive to it. Life has become a matter of doing rather than being. There's no margins, no room to breathe. It seems no matter how hard we work, we still feel like we're falling behind. Do you feel like that? When you get up in the morning, do you feel like a prisoner to the next thing or feel like there's a list a mile high hanging over your head? In the pressures of the daily grind, our hearts become swamped with feelings of fatigue, frustration, and futility. Our heads are spinning as fast as the world is revolving, if not faster.

JESUS UNDER PRESSURE

That raises the question: How do you handle the pressure of the adult world with all its demands and deadlines and the next thing that rushes at you like oncoming traffic? In Mark 3:7-19, we find an example from Christ about handling the pressure. Remember, the Lord Jesus lived under tremendous pressure. We tend to make the mistake of thinking of Jesus as a contemplative type, a monk like figure, who lived a cloistered existence away from the noise and commotion of everyday life. But that kind of image of Him is far from the truth, as Kevin DeYoung notes in his book *Crazy Busy*. He writes:

> *"The impression we get from the Gospels is that almost every day for three years he's preaching, healing, and casting out demons. Don't think Jesus is some kind of Zen master who does yoga and ponders the sound of one hand clapping. If Jesus were alive today, he'd get more e-mails than any of us. He'd have people calling his cell all the time. He'd have a zillion requests for interviews, television appearances, and conference gigs. Jesus did not float above the fray, untouched by the pressures of normal human existence. Our Lord did not sit around listening to harp music all day while the angels brought him heavenly bananas. Jesus was tempted in every way just as we are, yet without sin (Hebrews 4:15). And that includes the temptation to be sinfully busy."*[2]

So, how did Jesus handle pressures? Let's take a look at Mark 3:7-19:

> But Jesus withdrew with His disciples to the sea. And a great multitude from Galilee followed Him, and from Judea and Jerusalem and Idumea and beyond the Jordan; and those from Tyre and Sidon, a great multitude, when they heard how many things He was doing, came to Him. So He told His disciples that a small boat should be kept ready for Him because of the multitude, lest they should crush Him. For He healed many, so that as many as had afflictions pressed about Him to touch Him. And the unclean spirits, whenever they saw Him, fell down before Him and cried out, saying, 'You are the Son of God.' But He sternly warned them that they should not make Him known.
>
> And He went up on the mountain and called to Him those He Himself wanted. And they came to Him. Then He appointed twelve, that they might be with Him and that He might send them out to preach, and to have power to heal sicknesses and to cast out demons: Simon, to whom He gave the name Peter; James the son of Zebedee and John the brother of James, to whom He gave the name Boanerges, that is, 'Sons of Thunder'; Andrew, Philip, Bartholomew, Matthew, Thomas, James the son of Alphaeus, Thaddaeus, Simon the Canaanite; and Judas Iscariot, who also betrayed Him...(Mark 3:7-19).

Let's put this text in its context. While it doesn't look like it because it's towards the beginning of Mark's gospel, historically speaking, we are at about the midway point of Jesus' public ministry. Well into Jesus' public ministry, we see that He was a man who faced growing persecution (Mark 3:6) and mounting pressure (Mark 3:7-10). Jesus faced the imposition of the crowds and opposition from His religious and political opponents. On top of that, we have a reference to Jesus exorcising demons, which would remind us that His problems and pressures were not just natural but also supernatural in origin (Mark 3:11-12).

DEATH THREATS

The passage we are looking at is prefaced with a notation about the hatred shared by the Pharisees and Herodians for Christ (Mark 3:6). Mark details throughout his gospel a series of conflicts between Christ and the Jewish leadership, which makes Him a marked man. United in their hatred for Christ, religionists and secularists ironically join forces to destroy Christ. The point of interest for us is that this political and religious intrigue forms the background to our passage and reveals the opposition Jesus faced on a day-to-day basis. Talk about pressure! Jesus is ministering with a price on His head.

THE PRESSURE IS ON

In Mark 3:7-12, we are introduced to Jesus' ever-widening circle of influence and its accompanying pressure. Mark writes that a great multitude was following Jesus. Large crowds came from all over: from Jewish regions to Gentile regions, from Jerusalem and Judea, and beyond the Jordan. Mark states that great multitudes also came from Tyre and Sidon, which are not even within the borders of Israel. Jesus' ministry footprint was expanding, and a great multitude had come to see the things He was doing.

Because of this expanding influence, the pressure Jesus is under increases as the crowd presses upon Him. Whether you're busy at work, swamped by ministry, or have a few little ones scampering around your feet at home, I'm sure you can relate. Jesus is feeling so much pressure that He hints to His disciples that they might have to get into a boat and push out a few feet into the water before these people swamp them (Mark 3:9). Interestingly, in verse 9, where we read, "Lest they should crush Him," the Greek word for "crush" is the same word that is used of people trampling grapes under their feet in the winemaking process. There's actually a real danger here; Jesus could be hurt.

The crowd's pressing upon Him is leading to the possibility He could be crushed as large numbers of people strain to touch Him (Mark 3:10). This ever-widening circle of influence has brought more work and more demands Jesus' way. There was the press of the people, but there was also the constant spiritual warfare that surrounded everything Jesus did.

SPEAK OF THE DEVIL

Mark refers to the fact that Jesus not only cared for people physically by healing their sick bodies, but He cared for them spiritually by casting out unclean spirits (Mark 3:10-12). Jesus' fight was not just with flesh and blood, the Pharisees and the Herodians, but also with demonic forces (Ephesians 6:10-18). As is clear in Mark's gospel and in many passages in the gospels, Jesus ministered with the devil breathing down his neck (Mark 1:12-13; Luke 4:13). That's some pressure, wouldn't you agree? Jesus faced opposition both seen and unseen, both natural and supernatural!

As we see, Jesus was not some Zen master who floated His way through life without any problems or pressures. He didn't spend all of His days sitting in a cross-legged position looking heavenward in meditation. No, Jesus faced unrealistic demands from people, hatred from opponents, and constant spiritual warfare. Jesus knew what it was like to be tired, and tired of being tired. Jesus knew what it was like to skip lunch because one is so busy. Jesus knew what it was like to work against a prevailing wind of opposition. Jesus knew what it was like to have heaven open a window to bless, and at the same time hell open a door to blast.

So, how did Jesus handle the pressure? Well, in our text we see Jesus retreat to a quiet place (Mark 3:13), pray to His Father (Mark 3:13; Luke 6:12), and then delegate the work to twelve men called and equipped by Him (Mark 3:13-19). The next time you're feeling pressure and hassled, ask yourself, "What would Jesus do with the mounting pressure? How would He handle it?" In this passage, we see Jesus (1) *get away*, (2) *pray*, and (3) *relay*. Get away, pray, and relay.

1. GET AWAY

As we look at Jesus' model of handling pressure, we see Him get away and retire to the mountains (Mark 3:13). Jesus' life and ministry was lived under the gun of the next demand or deadline. So, in the context of mounting popularity, pressure, and persecution, Jesus escapes to a quiet place, a place were He could rest, reflect, and recharge. This was something He had attempted back in verse 7 in the direction of the sea, but the crowd had followed Him, as was often the case with Jesus (Mark 3:7, 19-20). This doesn't mean that Jesus tried to escape His problems or dodge His responsibilities, only that He recognized the need to take time away from people so that one can be effective when with people. People who take no time away from people ultimately become ineffective when with people.

Jesus got away because He understands what we often forget. We can advance through retreating. Military strategists tell us that sometimes the best means of advance is a strategic retreat; Jesus often followed that pattern in His life. If you read through Mark's gospel, you'll find several incidences of Jesus withdrawing (Mark 1:35; 3:13; 6:30-32; 6:46). The paradox is that Jesus kept going by stopping. We just keep going until we fall over. We forget that the best and most productive lumberjacks take breaks in order to sharpen their axes; if they keep going, the dullness of the blade will slow down their work. Therefore, you need to rest in order to run. You can do more by doing less. Listen! Sometimes the best thing we can do is to do nothing but rest, reflect, and recharge. Engagement, disengagement, then re-engagement: that was Jesus' pattern in life and ministry.

Jesus' retreat and getaway to the mountain provided Him with an opportunity to enjoy some physical *rest* and put Him in a position to receive some needed spiritual *revelation* from the Father. On the one hand, His body would receive renewed strength, and on the other hand, His spirit would receive fresh direction.

GET SOME R-R

Jesus' retreat to the mountain saved His life in more ways than one. Not only did He get out of the line of fire as it relates to the Pharisees and the Herodians who were plotting to destroy Him, but He also got away to physically rest, realign His body and soul, and to hear from God through prayer. Jesus pursued rest! Even though Jesus was fully God, He was also fully man and didn't deny or dismiss His humanity. Jesus needed rest, and so He made sure He got some. Jesus was running on empty and needed to refill his tank. He knew the benefit of getting away, a benefit He recommended to His own disciples later on (Mark 6:30-32). Vance Havner, the Southern Baptist preacher, famously said of Mark 6:31, "If we do not follow Christ's example to 'come apart,' we may, indeed, just come apart!"

Jesus always made time to get away in order to rest, reflect, and recharge. He kept His soul and body in balance. He always equalized His public life and His private life because, as someone has wisely said, "You cannot sustain a public life in public." Jesus would remind us that an effective public life requires an effective private life. We need to get away from phones, pressures, people and get some rest. And the purpose of that rest is to get alone with God, align earth with heaven in our thinking, reunite body and soul, and spend time in prayer and meditation upon God's Word. Our health, holiness, and happiness require that we work hard at resting and retreating.

Interestingly, a couple of verses earlier in Mark's gospel, in a controversy over the Sabbath, Jesus said, "I'm the Lord of the Sabbath" (Mark 2:28). Any talk of the Sabbath would remind us that God expects His creatures to break up the routine of work with rest. Life's divine rhythm is one of prolonged hard work broken up with strategic rest (Exodus 20:9-10, 31:15, 34:21, 35:2; Lev. 23:3). Jesus not only preached that but also practiced that. Consequently, we need to get rid of this foolish idea that the more we do, the godlier we are. That is foolish! As our Lord, and Lord of the Sabbath, Jesus would remind us to pursue and plan periods of rest. Physical rest is a spiritual matter.

In some Christian circles, to burn out is a badge of honor. But God doesn't expect us to play the spiritual hero or be a martyr to busyness. No doubt God expects us to work hard and to be diligent and fervent in spirit (Romans 12:11), but our fervor must be balanced with rest and retreat. We will do our best work when we also work hard at resting. It has been well said that we can do more by doing less.

YOU CAN BORROW, BUT YOU CAN'T STEAL

Remember this: You can borrow time, but you can't steal time. If you decide to burn the candle on both ends, you can do it, but not for long. You can borrow that time. You can skip sleep, skip food, forego exercise, and reduce your time with God, but that'll only last for so long. The reality is you can pull an all-nighter on Thursday evening. You can borrow that time, but you can't steal it. It's going to catch up to you by Friday night or by Saturday morning. God made us to function best within the rhythm of work and rest and to transgress that law of life comes at a cost.

REST ENOUGH TO BE GODLY

Our family is good friends with Keith and Kristyn Getty, who have blessed the modern church with fresh hymns and theologically rich songs. A couple of years back, we had dinner with them at Newport Beach, California, and as we were talking, this whole idea of rest and sleep came up. Kristyn shared that she was going through such a busy time and felt exhausted. She was a young mother and was on the road touring. They had so much going on in life and ministry, so much to do. And she said, "You know what, Philip, I've been feeling guilty. I need more rest than I've ever needed. To be honest, I'm sleeping longer, and I feel guilty about it. But I was helped in a conversation I had with D.A. Carson." If that's an unfamiliar name to you, D.A. Carson is one of the brightest minds in the evangelical world. He's considered one of the world's leading New Testament scholars. Brilliant as he is, he gave her some wonderful, down-to-earth, practical wisdom. In a conversation one day, he told Kristyn, "Take whatever sleep you need that allows you to be godly." That's practical and powerful!

We all need to hear that also: "Take whatever sleep you need that allows you to be godly." Again, we are being reminded in the words of this New Testament scholar that physical rest is a spiritual matter. The body must be allowed to catch up with the soul. Failure to do so will leave us frazzled and irritable and less useful to God.

A VIEW FROM THE MOUNTAIN

Mountains are associated with important times and turning points in Jesus' life. The climax of Jesus' temptation was on the top of a mountain (Matthew 4:8-11). He gave us His world-changing sermon on the top of a mount (Matthew 5-7). He was transfigured before His disciples on the top of a mountain (Mark 9:2). He preached the Olivet Discourse and gave us a view of the end times on a mountain (Matthew 24-25). He issued the Great Commission and gave the church her marching orders on a mountain (Matthew 28:16-20). And that pattern continues in Mark 3:13-19 as Jesus calls, selects, and commissions His disciples from a mountain, having sought His Father in prayer for wisdom and direction (Luke 6:12-13).

Jesus' retreat to the mountain not only afforded Him physical rest but also an opportunity to receive spiritual insight from His Father in the choosing of the twelve. God reveals His will to Jesus as He stands on the verge of calling the twelve and establishing the apostolic team who will continue His ministry following His ascension. Just as we can see further from on top of a mountain, Jesus encounters a new spiritual horizon on top of a mountain as He communes with God.

So, what's the principle for us? Jesus makes time to get away to seek the wisdom and guidance of the Father, reminding us that a work for God must always begin in the worship of God and in a word from God's Word. Jesus wants heaven to rule His movements on earth, and, most of all, Jesus wants to minister out of the overflow of His love for God, not the undertow of people imposing their agenda on Him.

Jesus understands that spending time in the presence of God best fits us for ministry in the presence of men. We retreat to advance, we first do less to do more, and we keep going by purposefully stopping. This is what Jesus is teaching us in His pursuit of some R&R – rest and revelation. Here Mark gives us this backstage pass that we might better understand the inner workings of Jesus' public ministry and pattern our ministry after His.

Think about this! Why was Jesus able to endure? Why was He so effective? Surely part of the answer to that question is the fact that Jesus often got away from men and the maddening crowd to spend time alone with God (Exodus 3:3; 1Kings 17:3; Isaiah 6:1). It's also a pattern that Jesus will repeat with His own disciples because, in verse 14, Mark tells us, "Then He appointed twelve, that they might be with Him and that He might send them out to preach" (Mark 3:14). And then we're given the list of the names of the twelve apostles.

WITH HIM

Did you notice that the first thing Jesus wants them to do is to be with Him? Before they're sent out as apostles, the Master invites them to spend time with Him. And surely that emphasis points to where all true ministry begins. It begins at the feet of Jesus. Martha learned that sitting with Jesus comes before serving Him (Luke 10:38-42). Notice again the order in Mark 3: choosing, communing, and then commissioning (Mark 3:13-14). The order is with Him and then with others. That is what made their ministry so powerful.

Jesus can do a lot with people who spend a lot of time with Him. In Acts 4:13, even the enemies of the gospel acknowledged this:

> Now when they saw the boldness of Peter and John, and perceived that they were uneducated and untrained men, they marveled. And they realized that they had been with Jesus (Acts 4:13).

James Edwards, in his excellent commentary on Mark, writes, "The simple prepositional phrase 'to be with him' (Mark 3:14) has atomic significance in the Gospel of Mark. Discipleship is a relationship before it is a task..."[3] That's a good word and a great thought. In ministry and discipleship, it is "who" before "what." Who we are before God will determine what we do before men (Daniel 11:32). The more time we spend with God in prayer, taking on His character, reading His Word, understanding His purposes and program, the more our time with men will be impactful and effective.

When I was sensing a call to the ministry many years ago, this prioritizing time with God was brought home to me in a powerful way. I had felt that it was time to leave my day job and to go to the Irish Baptist Bible College in Belfast. That was a big decision, which I shared with others for counsel, especially my father, William. On one particular evening at a Bible study at my home church, we had a visiting speaker named Dr. Fred Orr, who was an iconic figure in the Evangelical movement in Northern Ireland. He had established a great gospel ministry in the Acre area of Brazil. This wonderful man of God had tragically lost his wife to disease at the beginning of their mission there in Brazil, and yet he had by God's grace pushed on ahead. God used Fred in marvelous ways in Brazil. My dad, who had a great love and respect for Dr. Orr, softly elbowed me in the service and whispered in my ear, "At the end, you should go up and talk to Dr. Orr about your call to the ministry."

And so, at the end of the service, I did go up to him, and said, "Dr. Orr, I believe that God is calling me to pastoral ministry. I'm thinking about enrolling in the Irish Baptist College. Have you any words of counsel or wisdom?" In response to that question, he took me to Luke 6:13 [the parallel passage to our passage in Mark 3]. Dr. Orr read Luke 6:13 to me, which said, "And when it was day, He called His disciples to Himself." There was the word "call, " and Dr. Orr said, "Philip, do you feel called to the ministry? Make sure that you've understood the order. The call is to Jesus first. If you're going to be a good preacher, if you're going to have an effective ministry, it all depends on: Being with Him first. Do you sense your call to Him first? Is your ministry going to be about Jesus or about preaching or about you? It's all about Him, Philip. And so, young man, as you think about the call to the ministry, I want to remind you, first and foremost, that it's a call to Jesus – loving Him, looking like Him, living for Him. If you get that right, ministry tends to take care of itself."

Fred Orr was right and right on! Success in life and ministry always begins with God– His presence, His power, His plans, and His pleasure! Oswald Chambers wrote, "The only way to survive in ministry is to steadfastly refuse to be interested in ministry and to be interested only in Jesus Christ." Even if that has particular significance to men called into the ministry, does it not have something to say to all of us? How do you handle pressure? By carving out time with God alone and centering our life and labor on Him.

2. PRAY

Get away and pray. That is the Jesus way of handling pressure (Mark 3:13). While Mark doesn't explicitly state that Jesus prayed, Luke in his gospel does. In Luke 6:12, where Luke describes the same scene as Mark 3, Luke states:

> Now it came to pass in those days that He went out to the mountain to pray...(Luke 6:12)

This was Jesus' pattern. When faced with crisis, challenges, and choices, Jesus would often slip away to the mountains and pray for renewed wisdom, strength, and clear direction from heaven above (cf. Matthew 14:23; Mark 6:46; Luke 6:12, 9:28). In the context of Mark 3, as we noted earlier, Jesus is facing opposition from Jewish leaders, the press of the crowd, and the impending appointment of the twelve. In the middle of growing persecution and rising demands, Jesus keenly recognizes the need for prayer.

THE RELEASE VALVE

Prayer to Jesus was a release valve. When it comes to machines where pressure can build up, there's usually a release valve. Jesus shows us that prayer is the Christian's release valve. When pressure builds up and problems mount, and we don't think we can take one more step or face one more day, the answer is to pray. When life, ministry, and the home become overwhelming, you and I need to get alone with God, take a deep breath spiritually, and restore our souls through meditation and prayer (Psalm 23:1-2; Isaiah 30:15). In our desperation, we desperately need to hear from God through his Word, look into His face, and cast our burdens upon Him, knowing He will sustain us (Psalm 55:22; 1 Peter 5:7). As the old hymn says, "Oh, what peace we often forfeit. Oh, what needless pain we bear. All because we do not carry everything to God in prayer."

Jesus survived the clamor by protecting His time with God. For Him, there was no substitute for waiting upon God in prayer (Psalm 27:1; 13-14). Jesus realized you "can do more... once you have prayed, but you cannot do more... until you have prayed." Jesus understood, unlike us, that He was too busy not to pray. We think we are too busy to pray. Jesus thought just the opposite.

PRAYER IS A TIMESAVER

Just as Jesus handled pressure through prayer, we must learn to do the same. And yet, it's counterintuitive, isn't it? We tend to think of prayer as a bit of a distraction. It gets in the way of more important things, or we think we'll accomplish more by *doing* rather than *praying*. We'd like to pray more. We all want to grow in this area, but, let's be honest, prayer is often toward the bottom of the to-do list. But that's a major mistake.

We have got to stop telling ourselves the lie: "If I stop to pause and pray, I'll just fall further behind." Jesus is saying and showing us by example that just the opposite is true. Prayer should be our first response, not a last resort. Prayer is a timesaver because, in prayer, you get what God can do, and God can do exceedingly abundantly above all that we can ask or think (Ephesians 3:20-21). That's why Martin Luther said, "I have so much to do [today] that I should spend the first three hours in prayer." He understood that prayer gets things accomplished God's way, which is better than going about the day prayerless and doing things our way (James 5:16).

SPURGEON AND PRAYER

You and I can accomplish some things, but if we pray, we can accomplish much, because in prayer we get what God can do. Charles Spurgeon, the great British Baptist leader and preacher, learned this lesson. He said:

> *"Sometimes we think we are too busy to pray. That also is a great mistake, for praying is a saving of time.... God can multiply our ability to make use of time. If we give the Lord His due, we shall have enough for all necessary purposes. In this matter, seek first the kingdom of God and His righteousness, and all these things shall be added to you. Your other engagements will run smoothly if you do not forget your engagement with God."*[4]

That's exactly what Jesus is showing us here as He prayed on the mountain late into the night. A little bit more of God makes up for a great deal less of us, because with God all things are possible (Matthew 19:26). We must fight our natural inclination to demote the importance of prayer and trust in our self-effort. We have got to protect our time with God. Prayer is a timesaver and helps us deal with the pressures of life. Prayer unites us with God and connects our weakness with His strength and our ignorance with His wisdom.

THERE ARE TWO OF US

To go back to Spurgeon for a moment, Spurgeon was a whirlwind of gospel activity. He preached weekly in the largest church in London, he led a Pastors' College, he oversaw an orphanage, he traveled frequently, and he published books on a regular basis. The missionary David Livingstone once asked Spurgeon, "How do you manage to do the work of two men in a single day?" Spurgeon replied, "Have you forgot my friend? There are two of us. " Spurgeon was reminding Livingstone that through prayer and dependence upon God, he "can do all things through Christ who strengthens me" (Philippians 4:13).

When life is swirling around your head and threatens to swallow you up, say to yourself, "There are two of us" (Hebrews 13:5-6). On top of that, say to yourself, "I'm going to work hard, but I'm also going to work hard depending upon Him through prayer." Why? Because in dependence upon Christ through believing prayer, the less will always be more, and the small will always be bigger. As noted, Jesus and Spurgeon model for us the reality that prayer is a timesaver because through prayer God multiplies our weak and puny efforts. As

A.J. Gordon would remind us, "You can do more... once you have prayed, but you cannot do more... until you have prayed!"

3. RELAY

In our study of Mark 3 so far, we see Jesus get away, we see Jesus pray, and, finally, we see Jesus relay. What do I mean by that? Well, Jesus handled the pressure by retreating to a quiet place, praying for God's help, and delegating the ministry burden to others. He relied on others to help and multiplied His influence, namely through the twelve. He invited others onto His team to share in the responsibility. Read Mark 3:13-15:

And He went up on the mountain and called to Him those He Himself wanted. And they came to Him. Then He appointed twelve, that they might be with Him and that He might send them out to preach, and to have power to heal sicknesses and to cast out demons. (Mark 3:13-15)

Jesus selects twelve men, mentors them, and then commissions them to do kingdom work. He stakes the future on these men fulfilling His commission to make disciples who will make disciples (Matthew 28:18-20; John 17:20). Jesus brings these men on board to help share the burden of ministry and to increase Christ's kingdom influence. Notice the principle: When pressure is mounting, find others to lean on.

TOGETHER AND ALONE

When it comes to life's load, don't try to carry the pressure by yourself (Ecclesiastes 4:9-12). Strikingly, Jesus' chosen aloneness was also married to planned togetherness. The movement of the text shows Christ alone with the Father but then in the company of the twelve, through whom He will further relay His message and ministry. These are the men Jesus will pour His life into and then launch them on a global mission, as records the book of Acts (Acts 1:4-11). For Jesus, team ministry and shared life was one of the secrets to handling life's pressures.

Shared life and team ministry was the Jesus way! In support of this, when you study the gospel record, you often find disciples paired up by name: Peter and Andrew, James and John, Philip and Bartholomew (John 1:45), Thomas and Matthew, James and Thaddaeus (John 14:22). In fact, in Mark 6:7, Jesus sends the twelve out in pairs. When He sends the seventy disciples out, He sends them out two by two (Luke 10:1). Jesus put a premium on partnership in life and labor.

Life is a team sport. Life rarely works when we try to make things happen on our own. Others allow us to half our troubles, double our joys, and triple our possibilities. That is the beautiful thing about marriage (1 Peter 3:6), that is the value of friendship (1 Samuel 23:14-18), and that is the power of church (Hebrews 10:24-25). According to the Bible, renewal, relief, and release come in the shape of other people (2 Corinthians 7:5-7).

BIRDS OF A FEATHER FLOCK TOGETHER

The students of Westminster College must have been surprised when President Peggy Stock addressed the graduating seniors and began her speech with a bird story. She said:

> *"Yes, you heard me correctly. As you go forth from Westminster College, I would like you to remember some simple facts about geese as you wing your way through life. One, geese fly in a V formation because they have a 71 percent greater flying range together than flying alone. Two, whenever a goose flies out of formation, it soon feels the added drag and quickly tries to get back into position. Three, when the lead goose gets tired, it rotates further back into the formation, and another goose takes the lead. Finally, if a goose becomes sick or wounded and cannot keep up with the flock, two other geese also leave the formation and stay with the wounded goose until it either recovers or dies."*[5]

We have a lot to learn from geese, don't we? They remind us that two are better than one and that life is a team sport. The V formation of migrating geese reminds us that friends, pastors, church, spouses, family, and the gift of the Holy Spirit can raise the percentages in our life. They can help us to fly into the headwinds of life. They can enable us to better handle the pressures we face.

In our study of Mark 3:7-19, Jesus Christ shows us how to handle the pressures of life: first, get away; second, pray;

and, third, relay. So don't forget to work hard at resting, for you can do more by doing less! So don't forget that your busyness is not an excuse not to pray but an urgent call to more prayer! So don't forget that life is a team sport and God doesn't expect you to sing solo.

- **GET AWAY**
- **PRAY**
- **RELAY**

ENDNOTES:

1. Stephen Davey, *Nehemiah: Memoirs of an Ordinary Man* (Greenville: Ambassador Publishing, 2005), 181.
2. Kevin DeYoung, *Crazy Busy* (Wheaton: Crossway, 2013), 54.
3. James R. Edwards, *The Gospel According to Mark: The Pillar New Testiment Commentary* (Grand Rapids: Eerdmans, 2002), 113.
4. Michael Earley, *Pastoral Leadership is: How to Shepherd God's People with Passion and Confidence* (Nashville: B&H, 2012), 80.
5. Gary R. Collins, *Breathless: Transform Your Time Starved Days Into A Life Well Lived* (Wheaton: Tyndale, 1998), 137.